Planets

Mercury

3

LEVELED READERS

An Imprint of Abdo Zoom • abdobooks.com

Level 1 – Beginning
Short and simple sentences with familiar words or patterns for children who are beginning to understand how letters and sounds go together.

Level 2 – Emerging
Longer words and sentences with more complex language patterns for readers who are practicing common words and letter sounds.

Level 3 – Transitional
More developed language and vocabulary for readers who are becoming more independent.

abdobooks.com

Published by Abdo Zoom, a division of ABDO, PO Box 398166, Minneapolis, Minnesota 55439.
Copyright © 2019 by Abdo Consulting Group, Inc. International copyrights reserved in all countries.
No part of this book may be reproduced in any form without written permission from the publisher.
Dash!™ is a trademark and logo of Abdo Zoom.

Printed in the United States of America, North Mankato, Minnesota.
092018
012019

Photo Credits: Alamy, Getty Images, iStock, NASA, Science Source
Production Contributors: Kenny Abdo, Jennie Forsberg, Grace Hansen, John Hansen
Design Contributors: Dorothy Toth, Neil Klinepier

Library of Congress Control Number: 2018946213

Publisher's Cataloging in Publication Data

Names: Murray, Julie, author.
Title: Mercury / by Julie Murray.
Description: Minneapolis, Minnesota : Abdo Zoom, 2019 | Series: Planets |
    Includes online resources and index.
Identifiers: ISBN 9781532125294 (lib. bdg.) | ISBN 9781641856744 (pbk.) |
    ISBN 9781532126314 (ebook) | ISBN 9781532126826 (Read-to-me ebook)
Subjects: LCSH: Mercury (Planet)--Juvenile literature. | Mercury (Planet)--
    Exploration--Juvenile literature. | Planets--Juvenile literature. | Solar system--
    Juvenile literature.
Classification: DDC 523.41--dc23

Table of Contents

Mercury

Sun

Mercury

Earth

Venus

Uranus

Neptune

Jupiter

Saturn

Mars

Mercury is a planet in our **solar system**. It is the closest planet to the sun and has no moons. Mercury is the smallest planet. It could fit inside Earth 18 times!

Mercury does not have an **atmosphere**. It has a thin **exosphere**. It is made up of atoms bouncing off the planet. These are from solar wind and asteroids.

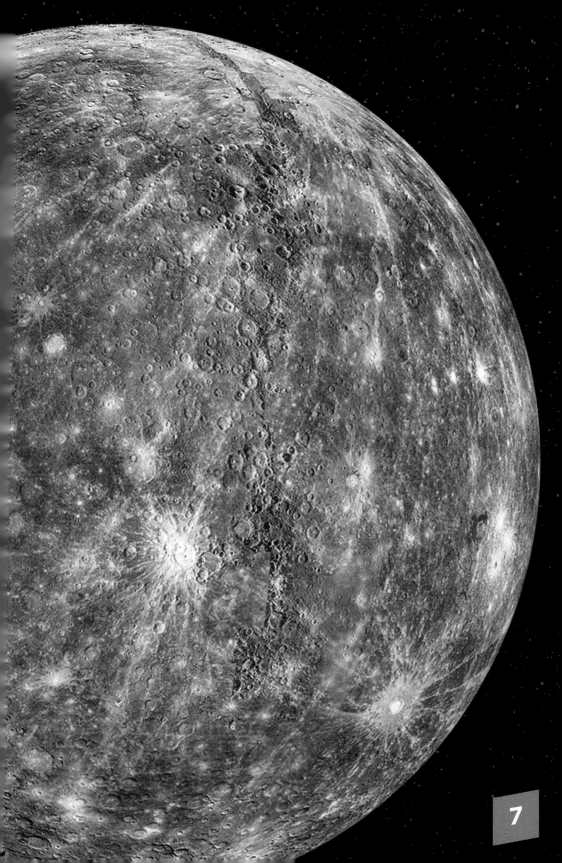

Temperatures on Mercury are extreme! During the day, it can reach 800 °F (427 °C). It can fall to -290 °F (-179 °C) at night. There are no clouds, rain, or storms on Mercury.

It only takes Mercury 88
Earth days to orbit the sun.
This makes for a short year!
Mercury spins slowly as it
orbits. One full rotation is one
day. One day on Mercury
equals 59 days on Earth!

On the Surface

Mercury has a core, mantle, and crust. The iron core makes up about 75% of the planet. The mantle is rocky. The crust is thin and brittle.

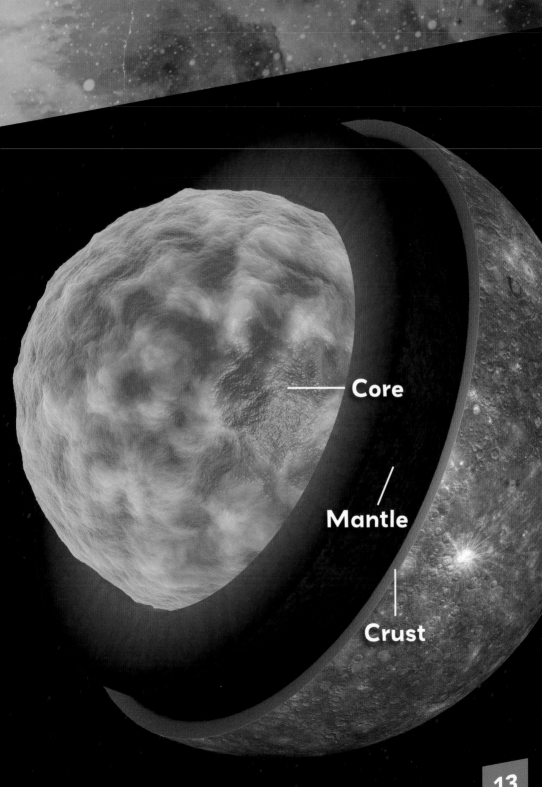

Core

Mantle

Crust

The surface of Mercury is dry, rocky, and full of craters. The craters are from asteroids hitting the planet. Mercury has valleys, ridges, and smooth areas too.

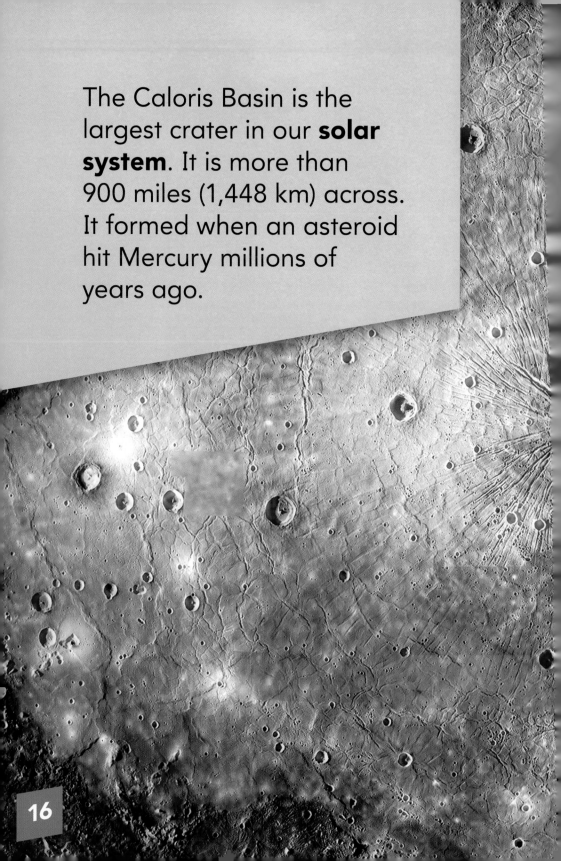

The Caloris Basin is the largest crater in our **solar system**. It is more than 900 miles (1,448 km) across. It formed when an asteroid hit Mercury millions of years ago.

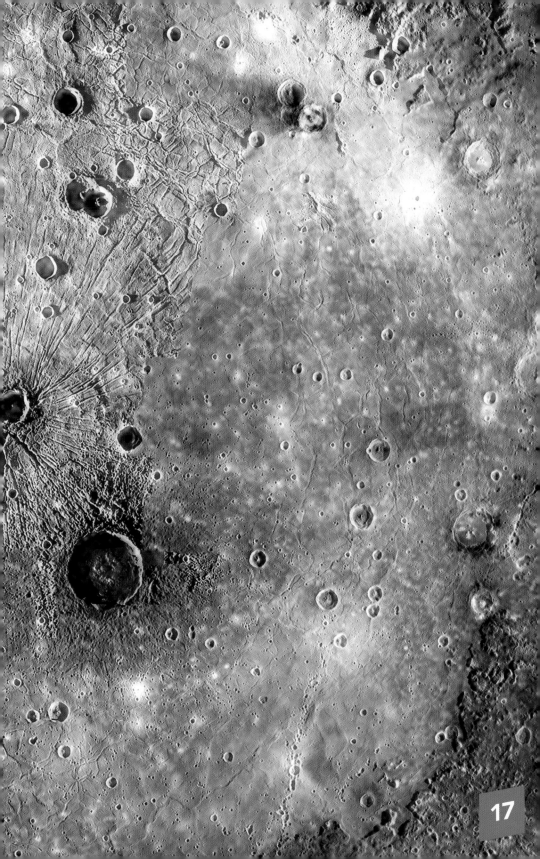

Studying Mercury

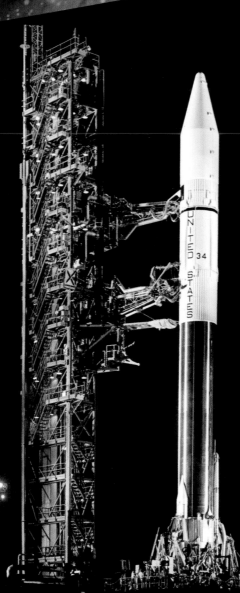

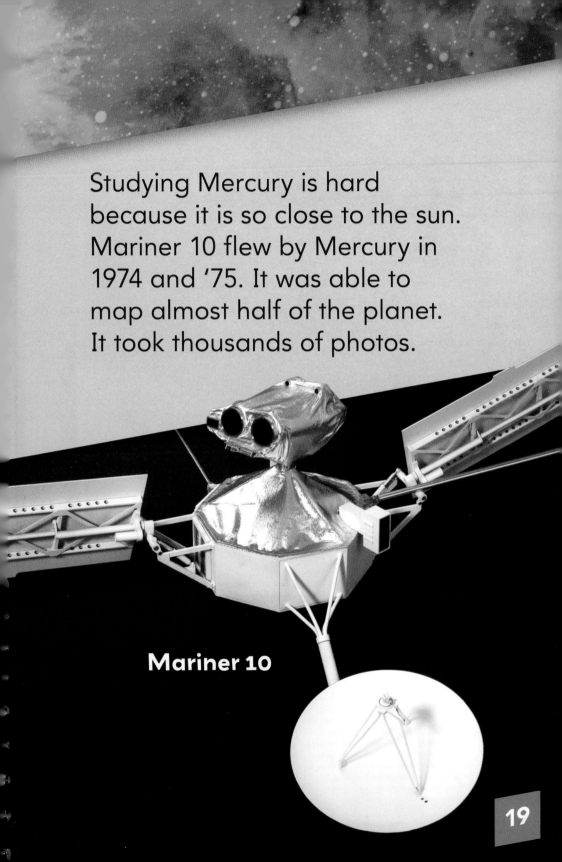

Studying Mercury is hard because it is so close to the sun. Mariner 10 flew by Mercury in 1974 and '75. It was able to map almost half of the planet. It took thousands of photos.

Mariner 10

MESSENGER reached Mercury in 2011. It mapped nearly all of the planet. Photographs show water ice on Mercury. Europe's *BepiColombo* will reach Mercury in 2025.

More Facts

- Mercury is only 3,030 miles (4,878 km) across. The distance between the East Coast to the West Coast of the United States is about the same.

- It takes 176 Earth days for the sun to rise and set on Mercury. The combination of the fast orbit and slow spin makes this happen.

- Mercury is the fastest moving planet in our **solar system**. It travels 30 miles (48 km) per second!

Glossary

atmosphere – the gases surrounding the earth or other planets in our solar system.

exosphere – the outermost, least dense portion of a planet's atmosphere.

MESSENGER – a spacecraft; its name is short for MErcury Surface, Space ENvironment, GEochemistry, and Ranging.

solar system – a system that includes a star (the sun) and all of the matter which orbits it, including planets and their moons.

Index

Online Resources

Booklinks
NONFICTION NETWORK
FREE! ONLINE NONFICTION RESOURCES

To learn more about Mercury, please visit **abdobooklinks.com**. These links are routinely monitored and updated to provide the most current information available.

We would love to hear about the ways you have experienced being "faithful with much." Please visit www.FaithfulwithMuch.com and share your stories of victory and defeat. Our mission is to encourage others in the area of using God's resources in the way He intended, for His glory. May the Lord move you to act boldly in your giving.